STEP-BY-STEP

MAKING KITES

DAVID MICHAEL

ILLUSTRATED BY JIM ROBINS

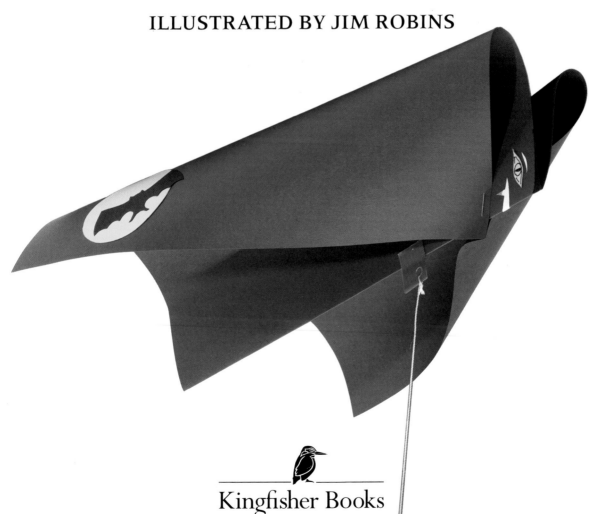

Kingfisher Books

Kingfisher Books,
Grisewood & Dempsey Ltd,
Elsley House,
24-30 Great Titchfield Street,
London W1P 7AD

First published in 1993 by
Kingfisher Books

10 9 8 7 6 5 4 3 2 1

British Library Cataloguing in
Publication Data
A catalogue record for this book is
available from the British Library.

ISBN 1 85697 1112

Designed by Ben White
Illustrations by Jim Robins
Photographed by Steven Sullivan,
 SCL Photographic Services
Cover design by Terry Woodley
Kites built by David Michael and
Anne Bates
Printed in Hong Kong

CONTENTS

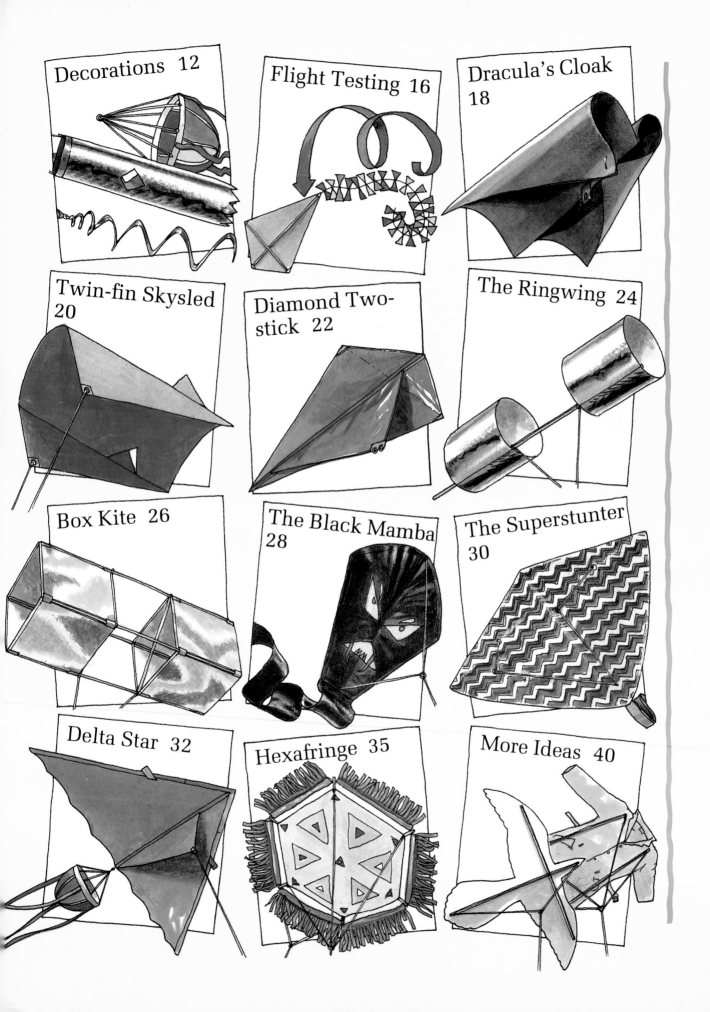

WHAT YOU NEED

To build most of the kites in this book, you will need to buy equipment from a specialist kite or hobby shop. You will also need some simple household equipment, and a good-sized working area – kite building takes up a lot of space.

Frame Materials

The *spars* or sticks that make the frame of a kite can be made from a variety of materials.

Bamboo is a traditional material, and is still useful for smaller kites.

Hardwood sticks can be bought from model and kite shops, as well as do-it-yourself stores.

Plastic rods are strong, light and easily bent. Bigger sizes come in hollow tube form, which keeps the weight down.

More expensive, but the strongest and lightest sticks of all, are those made from *carbon fibre*.

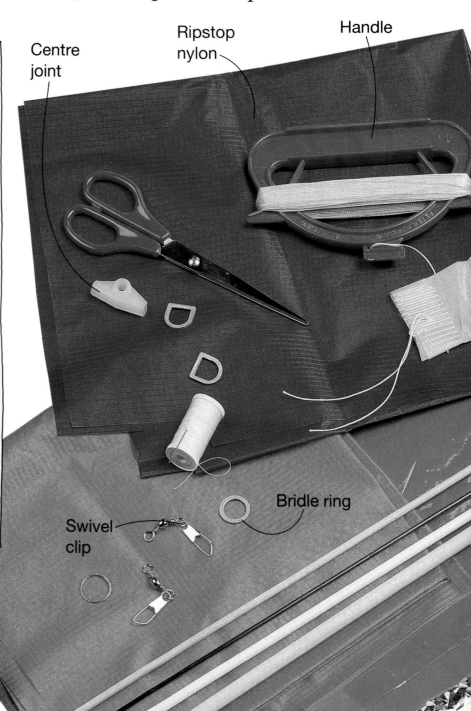

Centre joint

Ripstop nylon

Handle

Swivel clip

Bridle ring

Sail Materials

The sail of a kite can be made from anything that is light and won't tear easily. Light-wind kites can even be made from *paper*. *Polythene* is probably the best choice for beginners – it is strong, waterproof and can be repaired with tape. *Ripstop nylon* needs to be sewn rather than taped, but it is the top choice for the experienced kite builder.

Lines and Rings

Lines come in many different weights, from thin thread for light kites, to super-strong line tough enough to lift you off the ground! For your first kites, buy medium-strength line and a simple plastic handle. Later, you may prefer to buy a reel-mounted line. Buy aluminium bridle rings, or use curtain rings. A swivel clip lets you add a spinning tail.

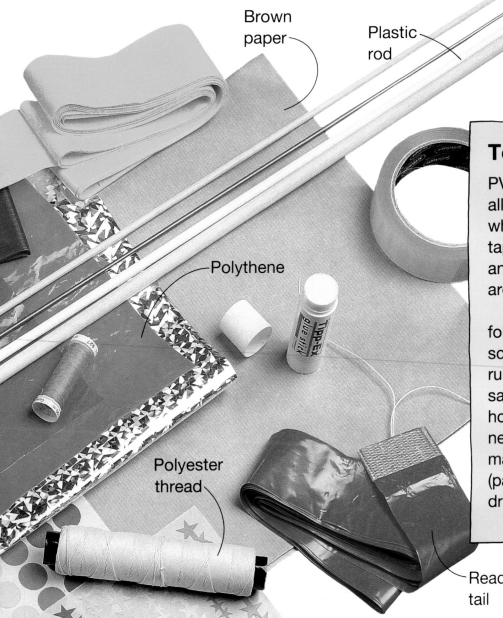

Brown paper

Plastic rod

Carbon rod

Hardwood rod

Polythene

Polyester thread

Ready-made tail

Tools

PVA can be used to glue all kite parts. Use tape when you can – invisible tape, waterproof tape and double-sided tape are all useful.

You will also need the following: a craft knife, scissors, a protractor, ruler, a small hacksaw, sandpaper, a compass, hole puncher, and a needle and thread. To make the Hexafringe (page 35) you will need a drill, and an adult's help.

5

PARTS OF A KITE

Although the kites in this book all have different designs, the basic parts share the same name. These parts can be found on the diagrams below. On the following pages, you will find everything you need to know about putting the parts together.

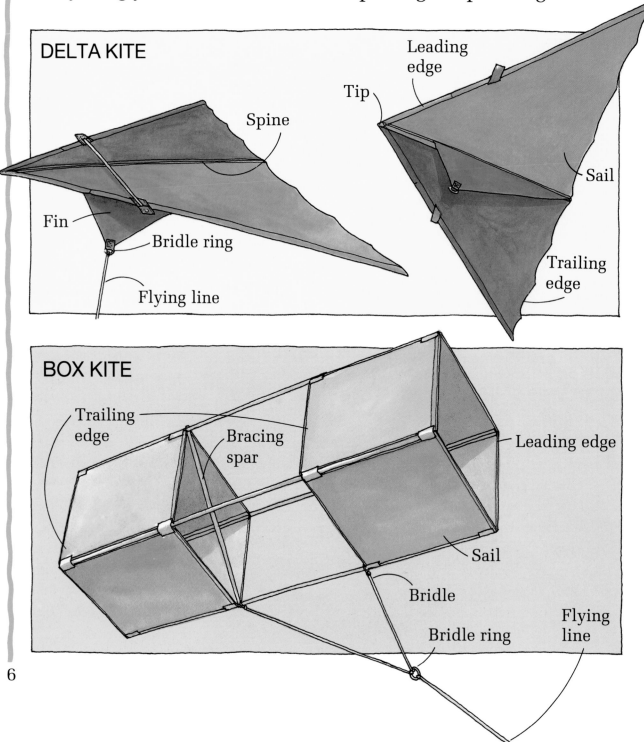

DELTA KITE

Spine

Leading edge

Tip

Sail

Fin

Bridle ring

Trailing edge

Flying line

BOX KITE

Trailing edge

Bracing spar

Leading edge

Sail

Bridle

Bridle ring

Flying line

MAKING KITES

Making kites isn't difficult. Follow the instructions carefully, and check your measurements at every stage. If you do this, your kites should fly just as well as the ones that we built while making this book!

Making the Frame

To make the spars, cut the dowelling, plastic or carbon rods into lengths with a fine hacksaw. Try to keep the sawing even and gradual – if you try to force the spars, they may snap. Use fine sandpaper to smooth the edges of the spar ends.

Joints

To join the spars, you can use strong twine, sticky tape or glue. For kites with angled sails (for example, the Superstunter on page 30), you will need to buy a metal or plastic bent centre joint from kite shops. Plastic joints are rigid, but metal joints can be bent to suit the angle of your kite.

Joining Sails

To join polythene, paper or card, you can use sticky tape. Overlap materials wherever possible, and tape both sides for extra strength. If you are using ripstop nylon, you should sew the pieces with a needle and thread. Overlap the edges by at least 10 mm, and try to make the stitches small and neat. For extra strength, sew two parallel lines of stitches, 5 mm apart.

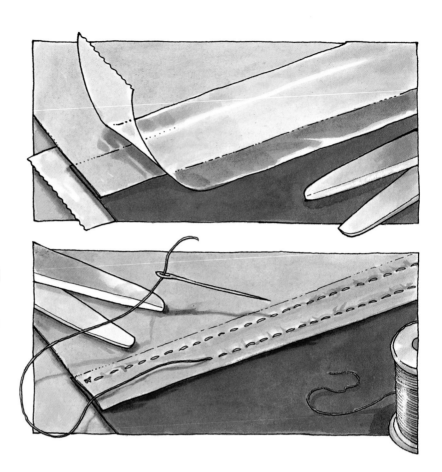

Making Pockets

The spars are kept in place by pockets at the tip, base and top ends. These are quite simple to make.

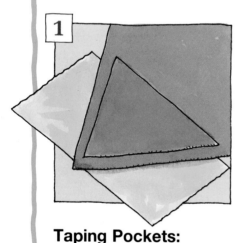

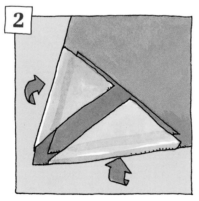

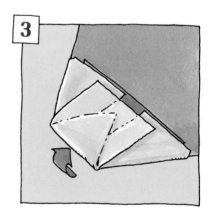

Taping Pockets:
Cut a triangle from tough polythene, to match the corner of the sail of the kite.

Use a strip of tape to fix the triangle to the corner of the sail, to make a pocket.

Fold down the tip of the pocket to make a straight edge. Tape in place securely.

Sewing Pockets:

Cut a strip from nylon, 90 x 25 mm. Fold in half, and sew as shown. Lay the pocket over the corner of the sail, so that it overlaps the corner. Sew to the sail – the x-shaped stitching will add extra strength.

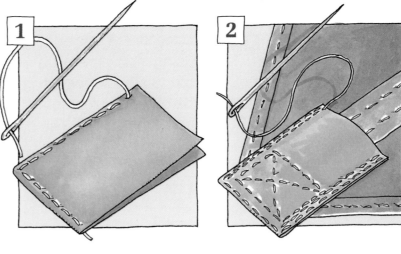

Bridle Ring Pocket:

The Delta kite on page 32 uses a bridle ring pocket. To make this, just follow the stages shown here.

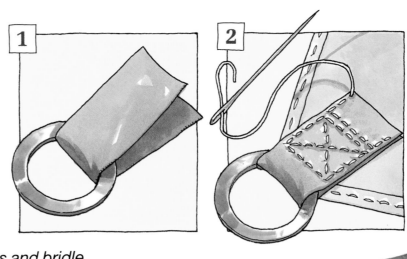

Below: The corner pockets and bridle ring pocket are sewn to ripstop nylon sails, using tough polyester thread.

Attaching the Line

When making kites, you will need to use two main lines. The *bridle* is tied to the kite at one end (using a bowline knot) and to a *bridle ring* at the other end (using a lark's head knot). The *flying line* is then tied to the bridle ring with a bowline knot. These knots are shown below.

Lark's Head Knot

Bowline Knot

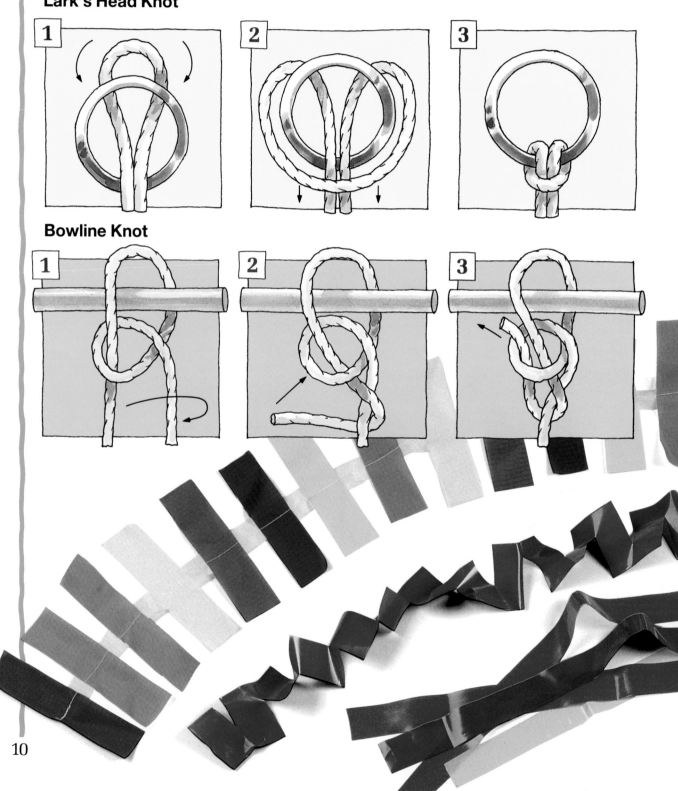

TAILS

As well as being colourful and attractive, tails have a practical use. They make a kite more stable in the air, and are essential for many designs, such as the Diamond Two-stick on page 22, and other kites with flat sails.

A simple ribbon tail can be made by cutting polythene or nylon into a long strip, 20-50 mm wide.

This tail catches more air than a ribbon. Simply make cuts all down its length with scissors.

Tassel tails are made by joining a group of multi-coloured ribbons at the base of the kite.

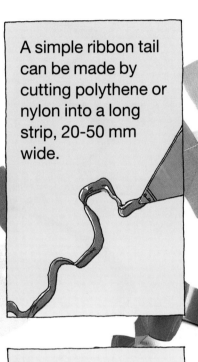
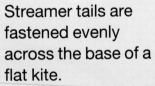

Streamer tails are fastened evenly across the base of a flat kite.

A flat tail uses one single wide ribbon (see the Black Mamba on page 29).

DECORATIONS

For added interest, try making some of the decorations shown here. They add colour and stability to the kite, and look spectacular in the air.

Spinning Helix

This looks hypnotically attractive as it spins round and round in the wind.

Using a dinner plate as a guide, cut a large circle from light card or shiny Melinex.

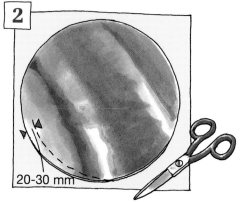

20-30 mm

Mark a point 20-30 mm in from the edge. Cut at a slant, to form the end of the tail.

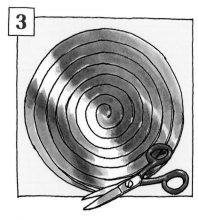

Keep cutting around in a spiral, until you reach the centre. Keep the lines 20-30 mm apart.

Attach the helix to the base of your kite, using a swivel clip (available from a kite shop).

Windsock

This can be made from nylon, polythene or (as here) from shiny plastic wrapping material.

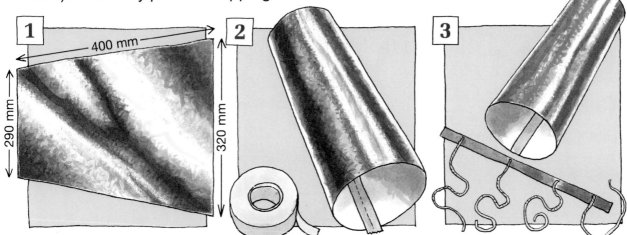

Cut out a rectangle from the material, making the sides 400 x 320 mm. Cut as shown, so that the trailing edge measures 290 mm across. Roll up into a tube, and tape

along the inside. Cut four pieces of string into 380-mm lengths, and cut 330 mm from a roll of sticky tape. Lay the ends of string along the sticky side, keeping the spaces

in between equal as shown above. Carefully roll the wider end of the windsock along the tape. Tie the loose ends of string together, and tie to the base of the kite.

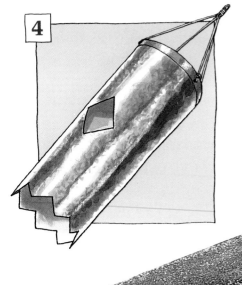

Cut the end of the windsock into a pointed pattern. If you like, you can also cut out diamonds from the sides, as shown.

Tailspinner

This tailspinner spins round in the wind, sending its ribbons flying through the air.

Making the Tailspinner

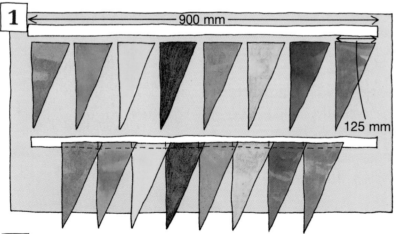

1 900 mm

125 mm

Cut out eight triangles from polythene or nylon. Make each triangle about 125 mm on the short end. Cut a waistband from ripstop nylon, 900 mm in length. Sew on the triangles, overlapping each one by 10 mm at the top.

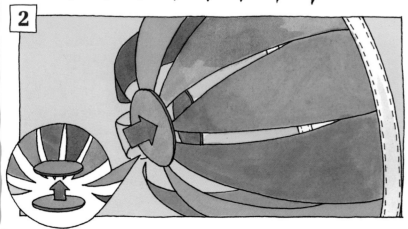

2

Cut out two tail discs from polythene or nylon. Use a compass to make them measure 30 mm across. Glue the tips of the triangles under the tips of one of the circles, then glue the second circle underneath the triangle tips.

14

3

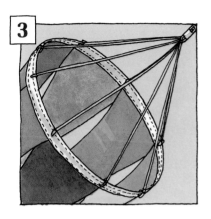

Cut eight pieces of flying line, each 260 mm long. Tape to the waistband, and tie the other ends to a swivel clip.

4

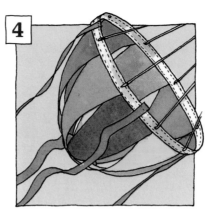

Tie or sew on four streamers made from colourful pieces of polythene. These whirl round in a spiral.

5

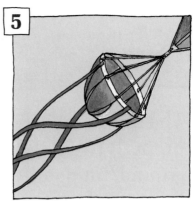

Attach the swivel clip to the base of the kite. Or, if you prefer, clip the tailspinner halfway up the flying line.

Climbing the line

When your kite is flying in the sky, what else can you do?
Try slotting this little spinner up the line, and letting go. . .

Cut out a 100-mm diameter disc from stiff card. Make a hole (about 4-5 mm wide) through the centre.

Use a compass to draw four 35-mm circles. Cut out half the circles, and bend up as shown. Cut the line A to B.

Cut 60 mm from a plastic straw, and cut a slit along its length. Glue into the centre of the disc at right angles, so that both cuts line up.

1

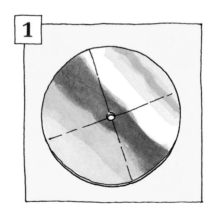

2

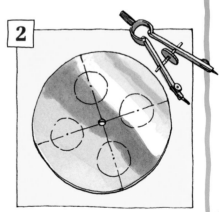

3

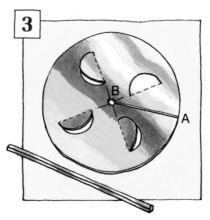

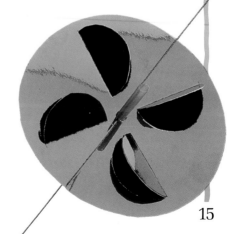

FLIGHT TESTING

The test flight is the moment of truth – have you built the kite properly? Will it fly, or will it crash? Will it even get off the ground? Hopefully it will soar like a bird – but you may need to adjust the balance first. Always choose open land to fly in, and don't try to fly the kite in very strong winds or when the air is still.

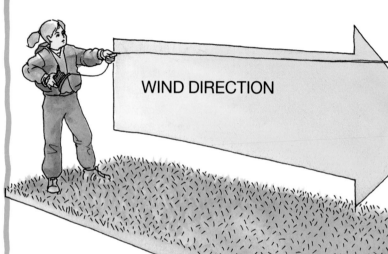

WIND DIRECTION

Launching is easier with two people. Unwind 6-10 metres of line, and pull it taut. Make sure that your helper is facing into the wind. He or she should raise the kite into the air, with the kite facing the wind. Pull firmly on the line – the kite should soar upwards. If it doesn't, try walking backwards or giving a few sharp tugs on the flying line.

Flight Safety

* Keep away from pylons, trees, houses and overhead wires.

* Use leather gloves if it's very windy. Line can burn the flesh if it unwinds suddenly.

* Don't fly kites near airfields, or at heights which may get in the way of aircraft.

* Don't fly in stormy weather. Lightning could strike the kite, and kill you.

* Don't launch the kite if people or animals are walking past.

16

Adjusting the Balance

A kite that flies perfectly one day may fly badly the next time you take it out – this may be due to a change in wind conditions. Try moving the bridle ring.

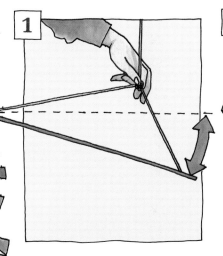

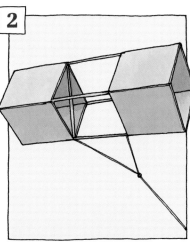

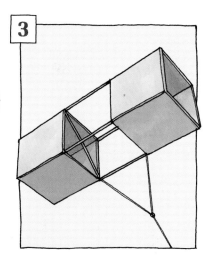

Before flight, hold the kite by the bridle ring. Adjust the ring so that the kite hangs at 20-30° into the wind.

Moving the bridle forward makes the kite fly higher, at a flat angle to the wind. This is good for smooth winds.

Moving the bridle backwards makes the kite fly at a steeper angle. Use in medium to gusty winds.

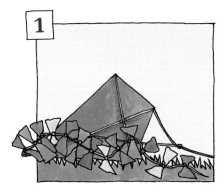

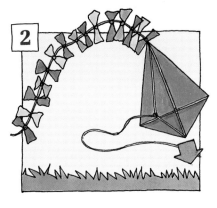

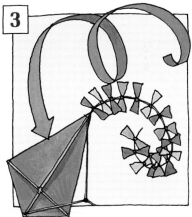

Trouble Shooting

Kite fails to rise: not enough wind, bridle too short, or tail too long.

Kite flies, then crashes: bridle may need to be shortened.

Kite spins or wobbles: add more tail.

Landing your kite

To land your kite, wind in the line on your reel. If the wind is quite strong, try pulling the line in hand over hand until the kite comes down.

DRACULA'S CLOAK

All kinds of simple kites can be made from paper. Dracula's Cloak can be made from plain white paper, but it looks much more sinister in purple or black! It flies well in a gentle breeze.

Instead of painting your kite, try cutting features from coloured paper and sticking them to the surface with PVA.

1

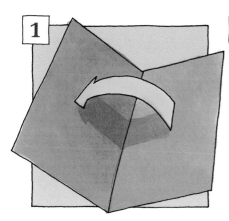

Take a sheet of A3 paper (420 mm x 297 mm), and carefully fold it across the middle as shown above.

2

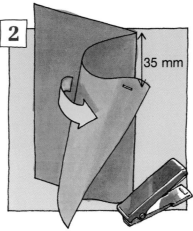

35 mm

Pull one side of the sheet round in a curve. Staple it against the centre fold, 35 mm from the tip.

3

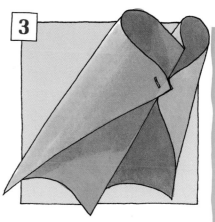

Repeat on the other side. Make sure the corners slightly overlap the centre fold, as shown above.

4

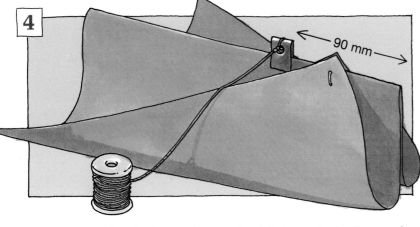

90 mm

Dracula's Cloak doesn't need a bridle ring. Just stick a square cut from thick tape to the centre fold, 90 mm from the

tip. Make a hole through the tape as shown in the picture, either with a hole puncher or a pair of scissors.

5

Use lightweight thread to fly the Cloak. It will rise in the lightest breeze, and hover menacingly above you!

Dracula's Cloak takes on a bloodthirsty look if you paint on some talons, fangs and a leering face! Use felt-tips on white paper, and poster paints on coloured paper.

6

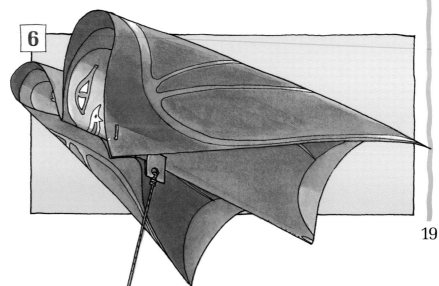

19

TWIN-FIN SKYSLED

Another good flyer in light winds, this kite can be made from paper or polythene. The one shown here is a good pocket-sized kite, but it could also be made on a larger scale.

Coloured sticky tape was used to decorate this Twin-fin. You could also use bright poster paints.

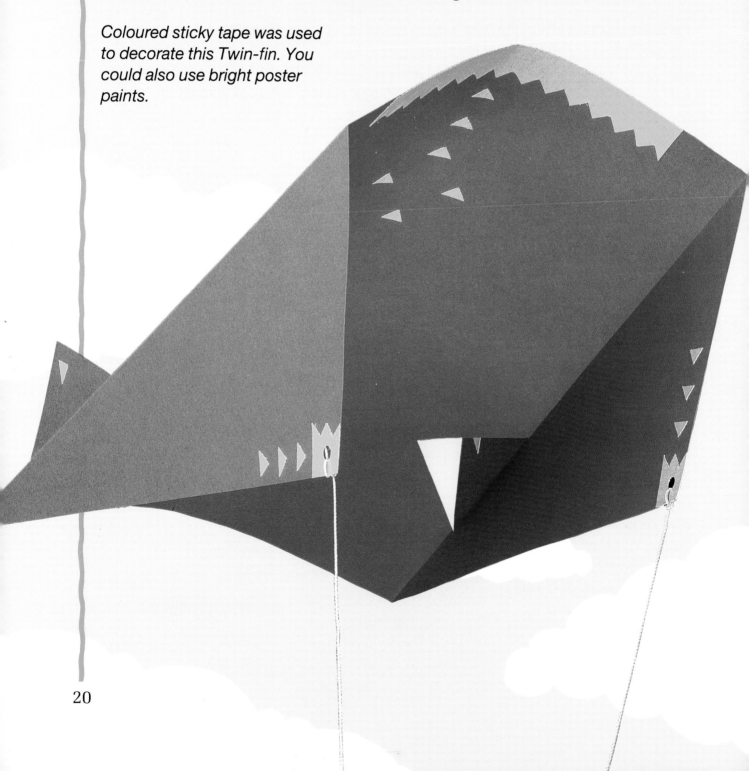

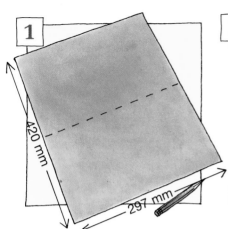

1 Mark a centre line down the middle of an A3-sized piece of paper. Don't fold the sheet, as this will spoil flight performance.

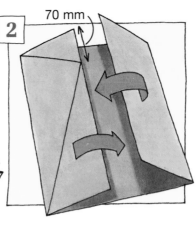

2 Fold both ends in to the centre line. Cut the sides in the triangle pattern shown – the tips should be 70 mm from the tip of the kite.

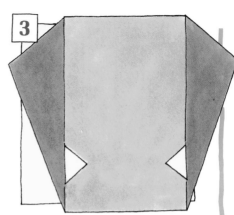

3 Cut out the two twin-fin stabilizers. With stiff paper they can be folded up. Polythene fins will be floppy until blown by the wind.

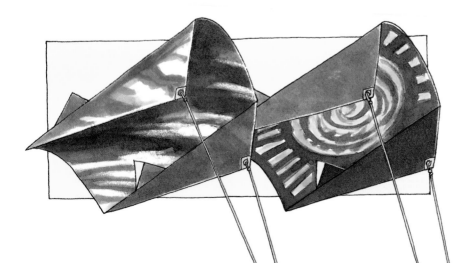

4 Strengthen the corners to take the strain of the bridle. It's simplest to use tough tape, and to make the holes with a hole puncher.

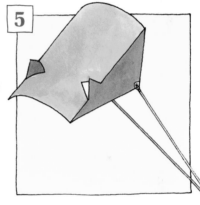

5 Tie on a long bridle, two to three times the length of the kite. Start off with 700 mm, and adjust if necessary.

Use Melinex or shiny wrapping paper to make a kite which dazzles in the sky like an alien spacecraft!

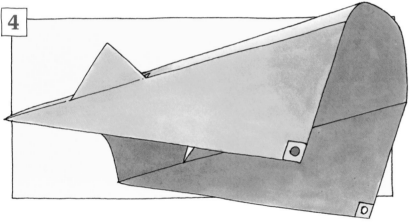

DIAMOND TWO-STICK

The Diamond Two-stick is a classic kite design. The one shown here has two bridle rings – use the top ring for light winds, the bottom one for stronger conditions. Add a longer tail if the kite wobbles in flight.

1

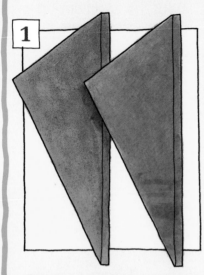

Cut two triangles from polythene or ripstop nylon. Make them the same size, and allow an extra 10 mm overlap on the spine edge.

2

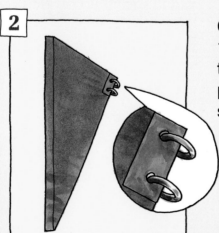

3

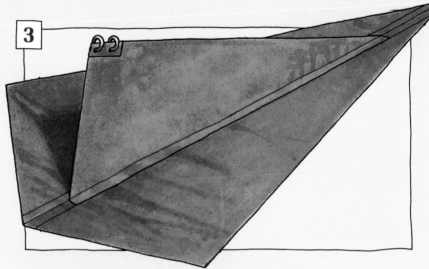

Sew or tape the two sails together. Join them along their longest sides, as shown above. Sew or tape on the fin, positioning it 90 mm from the tip of the kite.

Cut out a fin, allowing 10 mm overlap. Cover the corner with tape, punch two holes and slip on two split rings.

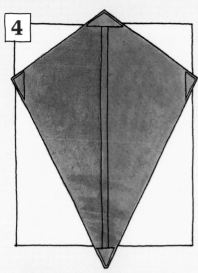

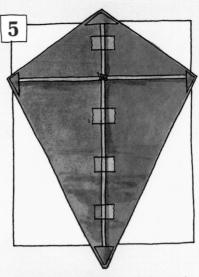

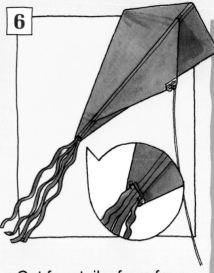

Tape or sew triangular pockets to the tip, base and sail ends. They need to be very strong, so use thicker material than the sail fabric.

Cut two pieces of dowel (6.8-mm diameter) to fit the kite. Slide them in place, and tie the join. Tape the spine stick to the sail, or sew cotton tape to the sail and tie to the spars.

Cut four tails, from four pieces of polythene each measuring 50 mm x 2 m. Attach two of them to the base of the kite with a safety pin. Add the other two tails if the kite isn't a stable flyer. Attach the flying line to the top or bottom bridle ring, depending on wind conditions.

THE RINGWING

This Ringwing was made from thin card and 6-mm diameter carbon fibre rod. It flies well, but needs a strong wind for a good lift-off.

1

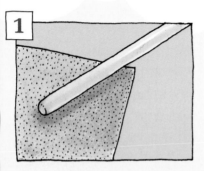

Cut a 900-mm length from the piece of dowel or carbon fibre rod. Smooth the ends with sandpaper.

2

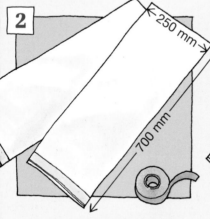

Cut two pieces of thin card, each 250 mm x 700 mm. Run double-sided sticky tape down one end of each sheet.

3

Fold round the sheet ends, to form circular sails. Rub down firmly over the taped edge to make sure it's fixed.

4

Use PVA to glue each sail to the spar, and tape in place. Try to make sure the sails are perfectly straight.

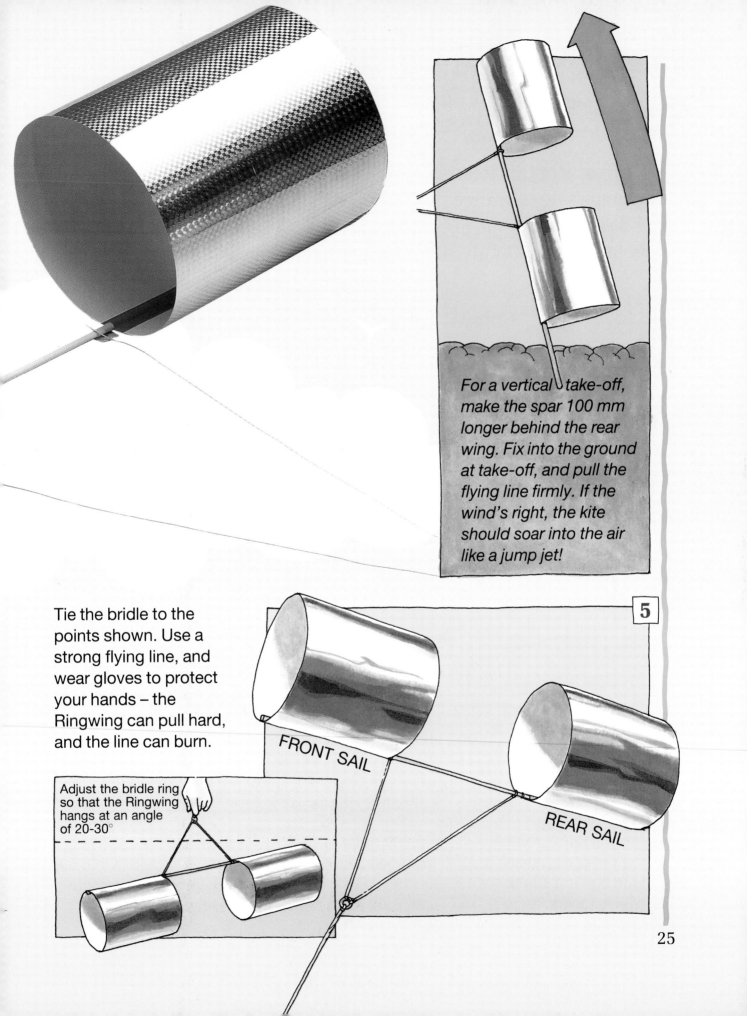

For a vertical take-off, make the spar 100 mm longer behind the rear wing. Fix into the ground at take-off, and pull the flying line firmly. If the wind's right, the kite should soar into the air like a jump jet!

5

Tie the bridle to the points shown. Use a strong flying line, and wear gloves to protect your hands – the Ringwing can pull hard, and the line can burn.

Adjust the bridle ring so that the Ringwing hangs at an angle of 20-30°

FRONT SAIL

REAR SAIL

25

BOX KITE

The sails of this box kite are made from polystyrene tiles. They can be bought from a do-it-yourself store, and come in standard sizes – usually 300 mm square and in packs of twelve. The frame is made from 6-mm diameter hardwood dowelling.

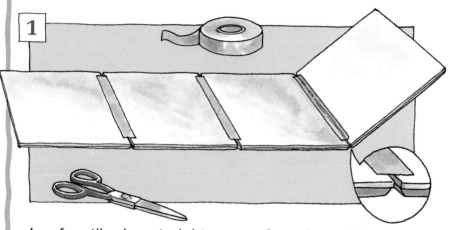

1 Lay four tiles in a straight line on a flat surface. Tape them together at the edges, making sure that the angled edges are face down. Then fold the tiles into a box shape, and tape together on the inside, as shown below.

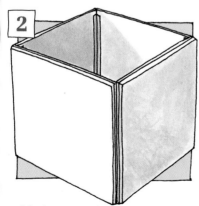

2 Make another sail in the same way, making sure that the edges are evenly taped.

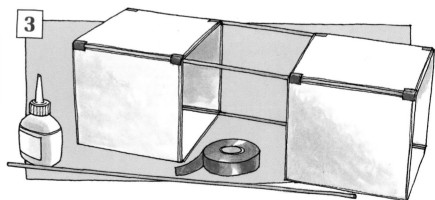

3 Cut the dowelling into four spars, each 900 mm long. Glue to the sails with PVA, and hold in place with tape. The spars should fit into the corners of the tiles as shown above.

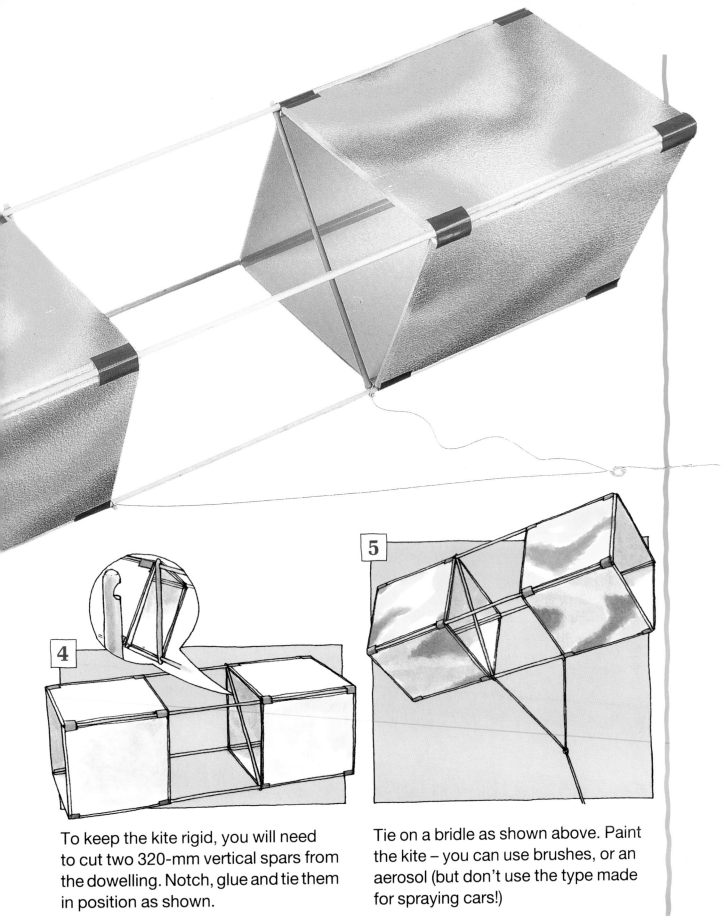

4 To keep the kite rigid, you will need to cut two 320-mm vertical spars from the dowelling. Notch, glue and tie them in position as shown.

5 Tie on a bridle as shown above. Paint the kite – you can use brushes, or an aerosol (but don't use the type made for spraying cars!)

THE BLACK MAMBA

The sight of the Mamba slithering across the sky is enough to send a shiver down the strongest spine – yet it's little more than a cunningly sliced bin liner!

1

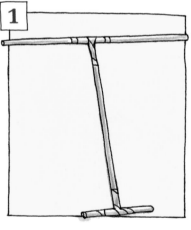

Cut three lengths of 2-3-mm diameter plastic rod to make a T-shape, as shown in the diagram. Fasten the three rods together with tape.

2

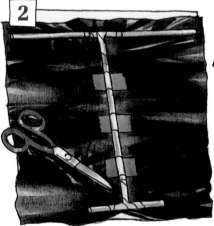

Cut open a black rubbish bag, and lay the frame on top. Tape down the spine and base. Trim, allowing 20 mm all round.

3

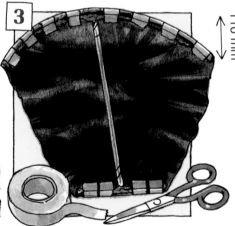

110 mm

Bend down the top rod, so that the ends are exactly 110 mm below the tip. Tape down the plastic, and trim the sides as shown.

Cut sinister features from coloured paper or polythene, and glue to the Mamba's face.

4

Tape down the sides – this adds strength to the kite, and prevents it ripping in strong winds, or when it is coming in to land.

5

Cut the rest of the bag into 160-mm wide strips. Tape them together until you have a long tail, and cut the end into a point. Tape to the base of the kite. Make two holes as shown, and tie on a bridle – adjust this if you need to improve the Mamba's flight.

29

THE SUPERSTUNTER

Take command of the air with this twin-line kite! The two lines let you climb, dive, spin and soar, but be warned – the Superstunter's a nervous flyer, and the slightest mistake will send it hurtling to the ground.

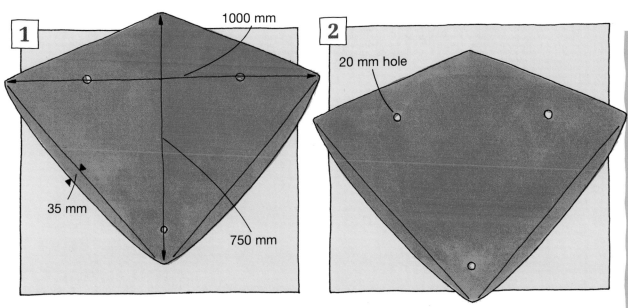

1 1000 mm
35 mm
750 mm

Draw this sail plan onto a large sheet of paper to the sizes shown. Cut out, and pin to a sheet of polythene. Cut out the polythene sail.

2 20 mm hole

Make three holes, 20 mm across, for the bridle. Then tape a plastic pocket (buy these from kite shops, or make your own) onto each corner.

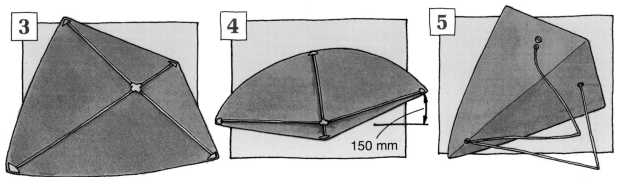

3

Cut four pieces of 6-mm dowel to fit the sail. Put into a metal joint, and slip the other ends into the pockets.

4 150 mm

To make the angled wing, keep one wing flat on your work table and gently bend up the other wing.

5

Two bridles are used for this kite. Tie them to the spars through the holes, as shown in the picture.

Tie on the bridle rings, and tie to two separate flying lines. Tails can be made by cutting old polythene bags into streamers, and taping to the base of the kite.

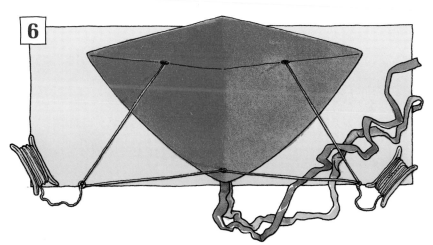

6

DELTA STAR

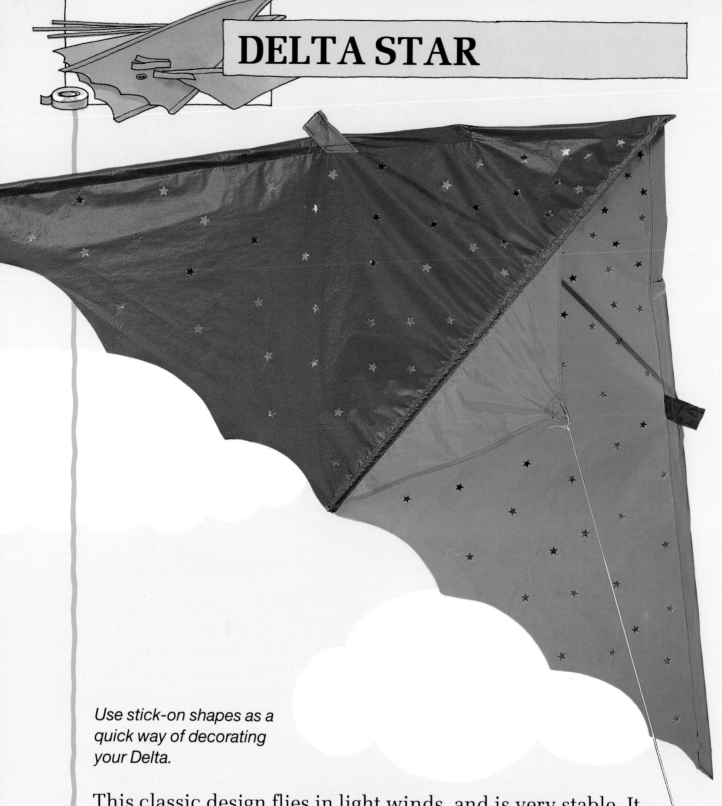

Use stick-on shapes as a quick way of decorating your Delta.

This classic design flies in light winds, and is very stable. It can be made from polythene and tape, or can be sewn in ripstop nylon like the one shown here. Add long pennants and streamers for extra interest.

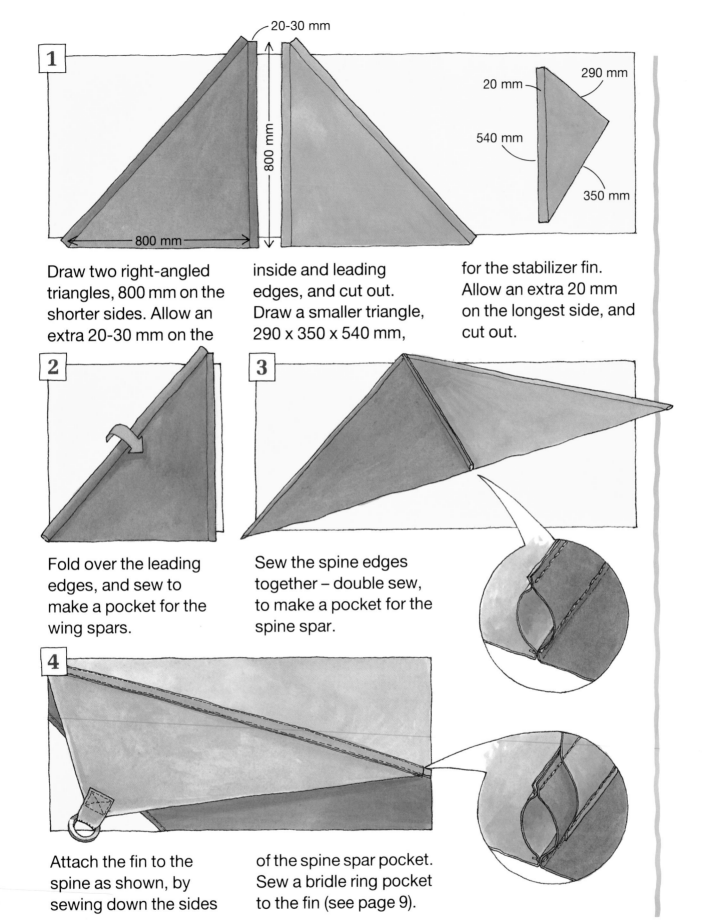

1

20-30 mm

800 mm

800 mm

20 mm · 290 mm

540 mm

350 mm

Draw two right-angled triangles, 800 mm on the shorter sides. Allow an extra 20-30 mm on the inside and leading edges, and cut out. Draw a smaller triangle, 290 x 350 x 540 mm, for the stabilizer fin. Allow an extra 20 mm on the longest side, and cut out.

2

Fold over the leading edges, and sew to make a pocket for the wing spars.

3

Sew the spine edges together – double sew, to make a pocket for the spine spar.

4

Attach the fin to the spine as shown, by sewing down the sides of the spine spar pocket. Sew a bridle ring pocket to the fin (see page 9).

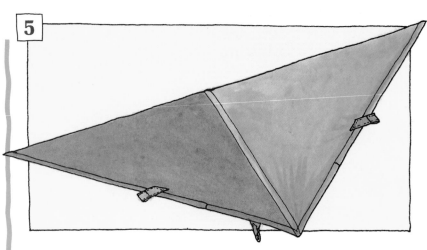

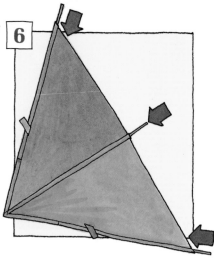

5 Make two pockets for the cross-brace spar. Sew the pockets to the leading edges, as shown on page 9. Make sure that the pockets are positioned 500 mm from the tip of the kite.

6 Make spars for the spine and leading edges from 6-mm hardwood cut into 825 mm lengths.

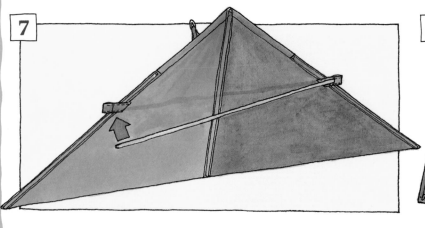

7 Cut another piece of 6-mm hardwood, 800 mm long. This is the cross-brace spar. Slip the ends of the spar into the two pockets you have sewn to the leading edges of the kite.

8 If you like, you could cut a scalloped edge along the base of the Delta, as shown above.

Decorate the Delta with stick-on stars, and attach tails to the base. You could also add a tailspinner (page 14), or even tie on a banner with a message!

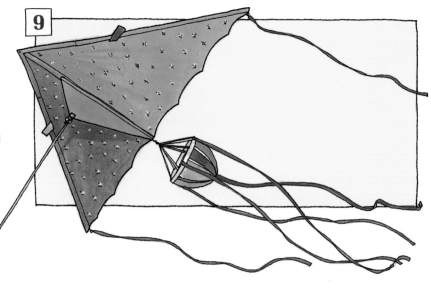

9

HEXAFRINGE

The design for this six-sided kite comes from Greece, a land of sea and sunshine. On a sunny day, its many-coloured fringes and long tail make it one of the prettiest kites you're likely to see. To make it, you will need to do some drilling – ask an adult to help you with this.

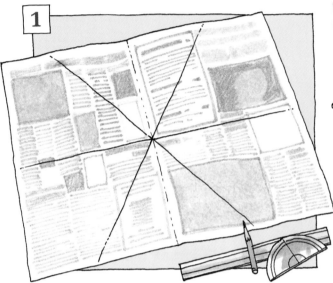

1

Draw the pattern shown above onto a large sheet of newspaper. Use a protractor to make each angle measure 60°.

Cut 5-mm square hardwood rods into three 800-mm lengths. Smooth the ends with sandpaper. Using a very small drill bit, make a hole 3 mm from the end of each stick.

Tape the sticks onto the pattern, one on top of the other. Make sure that the holes are on the sides. Then firmly tie the middle of the sticks with twine. Remove the pattern.

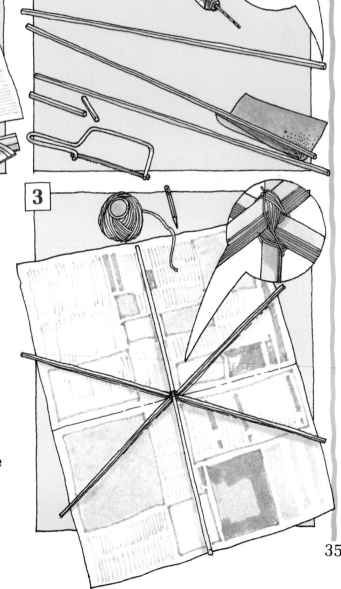

2

3

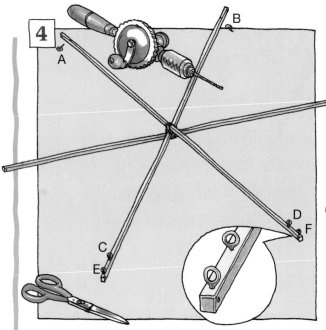

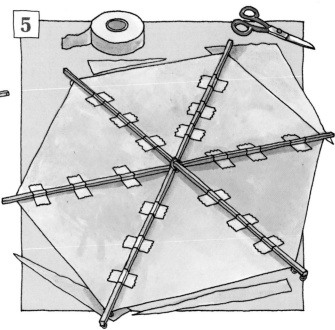

Drill four more holes, A, B, C and D, 50 mm from the end of the spars. These are for the bridles. Finally, drill holes E and F, 8 mm from the ends. These are for the tail. Screw eyehooks into all these six holes.

Tape the spars firmly onto a large sheet of brown wrapping paper with the eyehooks pointing down. Cut the paper into a hexagonal sail, as shown – the spars must be 50 mm longer than the sail.

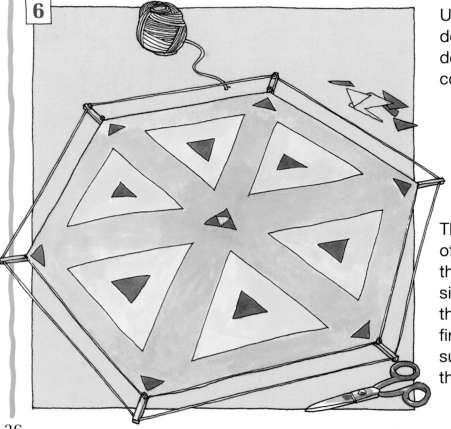

Use poster paints to decorate the sail, or glue down shapes cut from coloured paper.

Thread a long length of fishing line or strong thread through the side holes at the end of the spars, and tie firmly. This line supports the fringe of the kite.

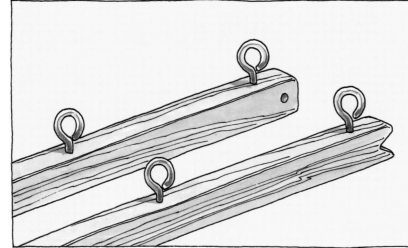

Holes and Notches

As an alternative to drilling holes for the fringe, you could try cutting v-shaped notches at the end of each spar with a craft knife. As with drilling, always ask an adult to help you with this.

7

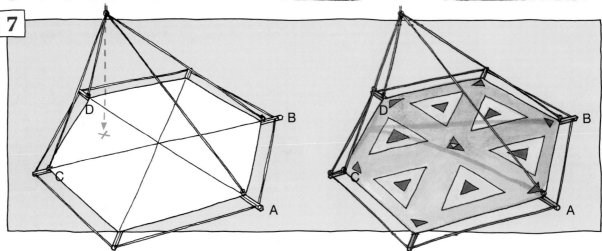

Cut four pieces of flying line, for the bridle. Tie one end of each piece to the eyehooks marked A, B, C and D. Then tie the other ends to a bridle ring. You will need to adjust the length of each bridle line, so that when the kite is held by the bridle ring, the four lines meet at a point directly above and in the middle of points C and D (see the diagram above).

Cut two more pieces of line, and tie them to the eyehooks E and F. Tie them together so that the lines run parallel to the edges of the kite.

8

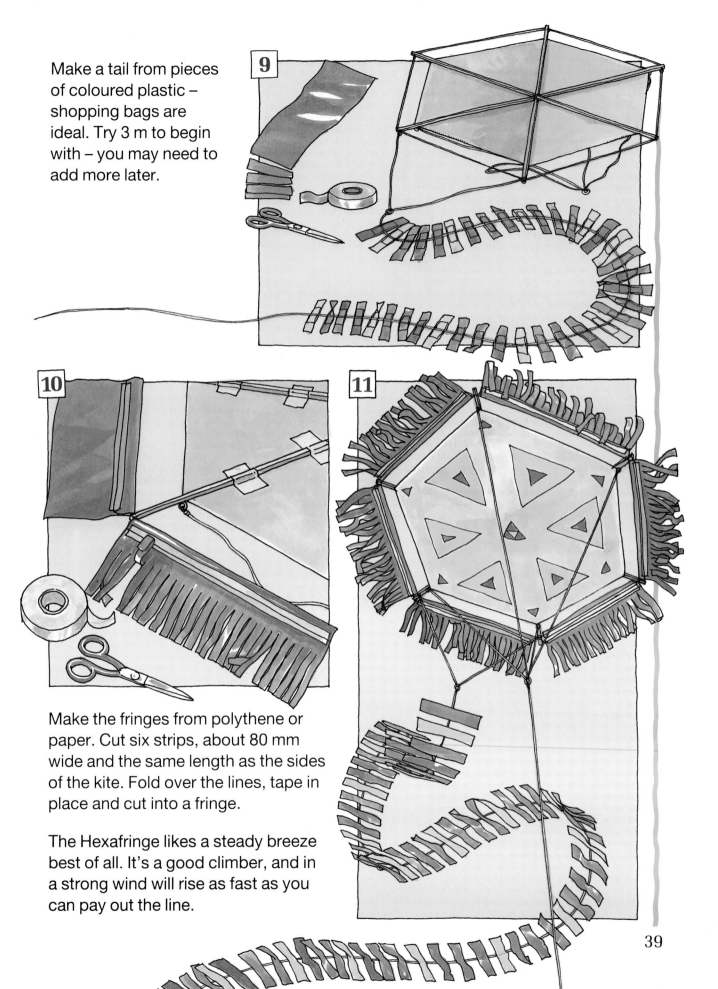

Make a tail from pieces of coloured plastic – shopping bags are ideal. Try 3 m to begin with – you may need to add more later.

Make the fringes from polythene or paper. Cut six strips, about 80 mm wide and the same length as the sides of the kite. Fold over the lines, tape in place and cut into a fringe.

The Hexafringe likes a steady breeze best of all. It's a good climber, and in a strong wind will rise as fast as you can pay out the line.

MORE IDEAS

Once you feel confident about making kites, you may like to try designing your own. In the meantime, here are a few more ideas you may like to consider...

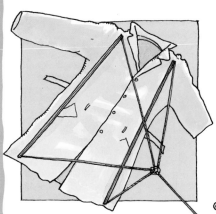

All you need is a thin plastic raincoat (the kind that folds up into your pocket), and two wooden spars!

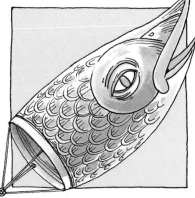

Based on ancient Chinese designs, this flying fish is little more than a decorated windsock!

Tie balloons to the ends of poles, and use stunt kites to try and burst them. It's harder than you might think.

This tiny kite is only 25 mm across, and can fly in air from a fan heater! Use the lightest sail material you can find.

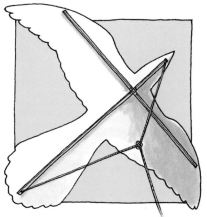

Kites in the shape of birds look superb. A prehistoric version could be made in the shape of a pterosaur.

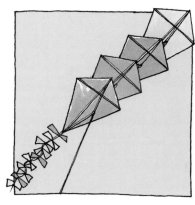

Flying a stack of matching kites is a popular sport. The stable Delta kite is well suited to stacking.